M000087937

Islamic Yoga

by Amir Fatir

Published by: Fatir Publishing Text is copyright © 2014 Amir Fatir

Islamic Yoga

The Mystic Tradition

The world's major religions were founded by people who employed mystic procedures to reach the level of enlightenment that enabled them to grasp the principles that have been passed down to us as religious systems.

A full comprehension of those systems is not possible unless we also engage in mystic practices which will unfold our own spiritual potential so that we may also fully grasp those spiritual principles.

Religion has primarily been presented to people according to the exoteric or outer court information. This information includes the basics on how to perform prayer and other rituals, basic tenets and emotion-laden stories (myths) which convey moral principles.

In the outer court, people are encouraged to listen to sermons about God and His prophets and to talk about the love of God and the love of His prophets. Few, however, are encouraged to experience God or to actually function according to the methodology employed by the various prophets. Such work is the business of the esoteric or inner court.

The Quran states: "They know the outer meaning of the life of the lower world, but of the Hereafter they are heedless."

While in the outer court people argue over such absurdities as "my religion is better than yours" or "my God is the true god and yours isn't," the inner court promotes unity because those who reach the inner court witness that unity and realize that god has always conveyed one primary message, a message that appears to be different because it came to men and women in different geographical locations and who were of different racial backgrounds.

Thus in speaking to people via their environment, God seemed to convey different messages.

People who reach the inner court realize that the principles are the same across time and geography even though those principles may be contained in different "bottles" bearing different labels. But the essence of the content is the same.

People who reached the deep religious wisdom of the inner court or mystic tradition are called yogis in the east, sufis in Arabia, shamans in so-called nature-based religions, Essenes in the Judaic tradition as well as Qaballists and many other titles.

Prophet Muhammad received the revelation of the Quran during an intense meditation session in the cave of Hira during the month of Ramadan. Islamic tradition says that the angel Gabriel appeared to him and told him to read. During the remainder of Muhammad's 23 years of life, the revelation that was given to him on that night came up in "main memory" as life conditions served to activate it.

A great portion of the revelation Muhammad received concerns the great mystic wisdom. However, few Muslims today are aware of the deep spiritual knowledge and terminology of mysticism and thus they miss the meaning of the majority of the Quran.

A study of the history of Islam after Muhammad provides the reason why so much of the spiritual wisdom of Islam was lost.

Until the end of his mission, the Meccan Arabs opposed Muhammad vigorously. It was not until Muhammad marched into Mecca with a massive army that the Meccans "submitted" to Islam, accepting Islam at sword point. They had neither studied Islam nor come to believe the teachings of Muhammad because of spiritual experiences or insight. They accepted the army and never got to understand the force behind Muhammad's mission. So the Quran says of the Arabs, "Say not that you believe for faith has not entered your hearts. Rather say that you submit."

When Muhammad died many of the former enemies of Islam became leaders of the Muslam ummat (community). One example is that of Mu'awiyya, the son of Muhammad's bitterest enemy, Abu Sufyan. During the khalifat of Ali (Muhammad's nephew and true successor), Mu'awiyya declared himself khalifah and set up shop in Syria. Mu'awiyya's rebellion reverberates today as the division between the Sunni and Shiite sects. The Sunnis were those who adhered to Mu'awiyya and the Shiites were those who adhered to the khalifahship of Ali.

When the Prophet died, Ali was supposed to assume the leadership, but while Ali and Fatimah, Muhammad's daughter, were burying the Prophet, the Meccan Arabs got together and appointed Abu Bakr as the khalifah because they felt they could control Abu Bakr due to his advanced age. After Abu Bakr died, 'Umar became the leader. He was murdered, possibly by followers of Ali. Then Uthman became the khalifah. He also was murdered, during salaat in the mosque. Finally, Ali assumed the leadership, but many of the Meccans, including the Prophet's wife, 'Aisha, opposed his leadership and civil strife broke out. Ultimately, Ali was murdered.

The false successors of Muhammad believed that with the new combined armies of the Meccans and Ansars (who were with Muhammad in Medina) they could take over much of the known world and capture war booty from Africa, Asia and Europe. On the other hand, Ali and his adherents viewed Islam as primarily a spiritual force for the good of the world. The materialists sought to keep Ali from power at all cost.

Like the Prophet himself, Ali practiced the esoteric mystic science that's today called Sufism. The Sufis wore wool mantles as a sign that they exercised complete control over their inner body heat (salaat) and could make themselves cool in the hot desert, even while wearing a hot wool mantle.

O thou wrapped up in thy mantle,
Arise and warn!
Thy Lord magnify,
Thy raiment purify,
Pollution shun!
And show not favor, seeking worldly gain!

-- Quran 74:1-6

The mantle worn by Sufis in Arabia is similar to a thin sheet garment worn by Tibetan Buddhist monks in the Himalayan mountains near China. The difference is that the Tibetans wear the sheet mantle as a sign of their ability to make themselves warm in a cold climate while the Sufis wear wool as a sign of their ability to make themselves cool in a hot climate.

This is an example of the essential unity among practitioners of the inner court mystic tradition across geographic distances.

Yoga

Yoga is a Sanskit word that means "union." It comprises a set of practices designed to bring about union between (wo)man and God. In Arabic, yoga is "Tauhid."

Tauhid is the yoga of Islam or the means by which the Muslim is to achieve taqwa (God realization) via unity with the Divine Supreme Being.

Say: He is Allah Unified
Allah is the Eternal, Absolute [Samad].
He does not procreate nor was He procreated.
And there can never be anything equal to Him.

-- Quran Surah 112

One of the goals of yoga meditation is to achieve the superconscious state that is called "samadhi." This is the same as the Arabic word "samad." This superconscious state results in union (i.e., "yoga") between the personal mind and the divine mind. When the initiate obtains samad she realizes that all that is is simply Allah altering the manifestation of His energy in such a manner that the illusion of separate objects and beings temporarily appear. But their underlying basis is Allah, i.e., the energy of The (Al) Force (Ilah).

Nothing really has been procreated or begotten because all everything is Allah and Allah has never been begotten. "He neither begets not is He begotten (112:3)."

The practice of yoga includes meditation, chanting words of power (mantas), postures (asanas), astrology, singing of special songs, special sexual procedures to achieve enlightenment, raising up the inner energy called kundalini -- all of which result in the union of the personal consciousness (jiva) with the All-Consciousness (Brahman). These practices comprise the true core of Al-Islam's inner court.

Meditation

The word meditation in the Quran has been mistranslated "reflect" in most English translations of the Quran. In many places the Quran states, "Here are signs for those who meditate."

Meditation is the method used to link the personal consciousness with the Divine Consciousness.

Mantras

A mantra is a word of power that is used to "download" the divine attribute that's associated with a particular mantra. In the Quran, mantras are called "dhikrs." Mantras are words of power in that they do not convey meaning, they convey power. These words on power are called kalimaat (words or letters) in the Quran.

Then Adam learned letters from his Lord.

-- Quran 2:37

The repetition of such kalimats is the practice of dhikr. The Egyptian word for words of power is "heka." This is written "haqqa" in the Quran and is usually translated "truth" in such verses as "Allah created the heavens and the earth with the truth [haqqa]."

He created the heavens and the earth with the Haqqi.

-- Quran 39:5

But what does this mean? Surah 69 of the Quran suggests that people would be misinformed of what the Haqqa truly is: "The Haqqa! What is the Haqqa? And what will convey to you just what the Haqqa is" (69:1-3).

Allah created the universe by means of a Logos or Word of Power (Haqqa). The process is discussed in the Bible, St. John, where it ways, "In the beginning was the word and the word was with god and the word was

God." John says, "all things were created by him, i.e., by the word or Logos.

Allah says "Be and it becomes." This is the function of a word of power (Logos, Haqqa, Mantra or Heka).

The divine mantra carries the same vibration as God Himself for God is an energy gestalt and all energy vibrates and everything that vibrates also creates a sound. And if you can create the sound, you can create the energy field (spirit or deity) associated with the sound. So in chanting a word of power you are activating in yourself the God faculty or characteristic and power of the being (God) associated with the sound.

This sound then transforms your consciousness into a replica of the divine attribute associated with the sound vibration. The Quran says, "Allah will never cease to change your forms again and again in forms that you know not."

Mantras are the "names" Adam used to make the angels prostrate in Surah 2:31 of the Quran.

The components of the mantras are the letters themselves. In Sanskrit there are 50 letters which form the elements of the yogic mantra system. These 50 sound powers are codified in the Quran as 50,000 years.

The angels and the spirit ascend unto Him in a Day the measure whereof is (as) fifty thousand years.

-- Quran 70:4

There are 28 letters in the Arabic language. They accord with the 28 constellations of Taoism. There is a 29th letter (Hamza) which is actually the same as Alif (the letter A).

The yogis teach that the original sound of the breath is "Humsah." They say that the natural sound of inhalation is "Hum" and exhalation is "sah." This "humsah" is called "the swan." It actually conceals the Egyptian deities (principles) Hu and Sa which stand for divine will and consciousness.

Published by: Fatir Publishing Text is copyright © 2014 Amir Fatir

Fourteen Mystic letters (muqatta'aat) are featured preceding 29 Surahs of the Quran. These 14 letters comprise the primary mantric system in Islam.

Repetition of a mantra in a trance state gives the mantra the power to transform your spirit and create you anew in "a form that you know not." Mantic repetition is called "jappa" in yoga and "Dhkr" in Islam.

Astrology

The root religious science is astrology. There are several branches of astrology including medical, natal, predictive, horary, financial, political (mundane) and spiritual.

Astrology is a cosmological language system that provides a holistic view of man and creation.

The modern scholars respect astronomy, but have relegated astrology to a "pseudo-science." Many laypeople accept that view without having conducted the slightest study of astrology. They have merely accepted the prejudices of the "scholars" without conducting any investigation of their own.

Astronomy and astrology were originally one and the same. All the great astronomers were also astrologers. While astronomy provides knowledge of the physical movement and gravitational affects of celestial bodies, astrology is necessary to understand their behavioral (i.e., spiritual) effects.

As religion and science were once united and were then split apart, so also were astronomy and astrology one interdependent spiritual-science system.

Split not up your Way (Diyn) into sects.
-- Quran

The influence of astrology on religion is evidenced in the emphasis upon the numbers seven and twelve. Seven is the number representing the seven "personal planets" of our solar system and twelve is the number representing the 12 signs. The seven personal planets are Sun, Moon,

Mercury, Venus, Mars, Jupiter and Saturn. The 12 signs are the well-known signs of the zodiac.

We have placed above you seven paths
The seven oft-repeated.
Allah created the seven heavens

The 12 zodiacal signs in religion is encoded as the 12 disciples of Jesus, the 12 tribes of Ishmael and Israel and as the 12 wives of the Prophet Muhammad.

The seven chakras of yoga radiate the energies of the seven planets and they are often alluded to when the scripture speaks of "seven heavens."

Throughout the Quran astrological principles are alluded to.

They ask thee concerning the New Moons.
Say: they are signs for the humanity

--Quran 2:189

The New Moon signs refer to the mass or global effect the angles made by the New Moon to the other planets has upon large numbers of people or regions. For example, when the Exxon Valdeze crashed down some years ago, spilling oil across the beaches, the New Moon made a quincunx (150 degree) angle to Neptune, the planet ruling the ocean and also ruling oil. The spilling of the oil from the Valdeze had effect on a global level, not only upon the physical ocean, but upon the oil industry, upon life in the region and upon shipping. Interestingly, the Valdeze captain was said to have been intoxicated and Neptune also rules over alcoholic beverages and drugs.

The hard angles such as inconjuncts (150o), squares (90o) and oppositions (180o) portend difficult effects from the New Moons.

By the stars they are guided

-- Holy Quran 16:16

Published by: Fatir Publishing Text is copyright © 2014 Amir Fatir

The above verse clearly indicates that humans are guided and directed by the stars. This refers not only to pilots of ships, but more so to initiates who can read the messages of the stars and planets.

And the Sun and Moon are joined together.

-- Quran 75:9

The above verse refers to the conjunction of the Sun and Moon or the period in which they are 0o apart. Within spiritual work, the ida nadi is regarded as lunar and the pingala is regarded as solar. In kundalini work, the initiate develops the ability to unite the energy of the two at the brow of his forehead (3rd eye) which results in his going into a deep trance. That is what is meant by the sight becoming dazed.

The union of the ida and pingala nadis at the brow (ajna chakra) is important in spiritual work in various systems around the world. For example, the ancient Egyptians referred to these two nadis as Uatchet (pingala) and Nekhebet (ida).

During embalming ceremonies, the priest states:

The goddess Uatchet cometh unto thee in the form of
the living Uraeus, to anoint thy head with their flames.
She riseth up on the left side of thy head, and she shineth
from the right side of thy temples without speech; they
rise up on thy head during each and every hour of the day,
even as they do for their father Ra, and through them the
terror which thou inspirest in the holy spirits is increased,
and because Uatchet and Nekhebet rise up on thy head,
and because thy brow becometh the portion of thy head
whereon they establish themselves, even as they do
upon the brow of Ra, and because they never leave thee,
awe of thee striketh into the souls which are made perfect.

The "living Uraeus" is the ajna chakra which is represented by the Egyptians as the snake (kundalini) protruded from a tiara around the forehead. "She shineth from the right side of thy temples without speech" because the right brain hemisphere is speechless. It is the seat of visual or graphic communication. When these two nadis (Uatchet and Nekhebet)

Published by: Fatir Publishing Text is copyright © 2014 Amir Fatir

are joined at the brow, the initiate (so-called mummy) is able to function as a "spirit-soul." This passage also deals with the principles of zodiacal hours, for which see my "Fitrah Astrology I: The 14 Kau of Ra."

So nay, I swear by the ruddy glow of sunset and the night
and it's homing and the Moon in its fullness, ye shall
surely travel from stage to stage.

- Quran 84:16-19

The full moon is one of the best times to meditate to reach deep trance. It also affords the meditator the possibility of travelling outside her body and ascending to other stages of reality.

By the sky containing the zodiacal signs.
-- Quran 85:1

This verse is a clear reference, even as oath, invoking the entire zodiac. It is impossible to say that astrology has no place in Islam when the Quran is so replete with references to astrology.

And we certainly placed the zodiacal signs in the heavens
and we beautified them to the lookers [i.e. astronomers].

--Quran 15:16

The Bible also refers to astrological principles and much of the wisdom of the Bible is coded in language that is impossible to decipher without an understanding of astrology.

Each "son of Israel" is a code for an astrological sign. For example, the Genesis says "Judah shall be a lion." This refers to the sign Leo.

The New Testament speaks of "signs in the sun, moon and the stars." Not only is this a prophecy of the coming of Islam -- whose emblem is the Sun, Moon and Star -- but it is also an indication of the importance of astrology in comprehending Jesus' work and mission.

Ezekiel, Daniel and the Book of Revelation speak of "beasts" or four "living creatures" who are symbols of Taurus, Aquarius, Scorpio and Leo. The

Published by: Fatir Publishing Text is copyright © 2014 Amir Fatir

"morning star," Lucifer, referred to in Isaiah, is a reference to the planet Venus and the destructive effects a negatively expressed Venus can have on the individual.

The "animals" Adam named in Genesis refer to the circle of animals or zodiac.

6 x 6 x 6 = 126.
1 x 2 x 6 = 12 the number of zodiacal signs

Because the zodiac is a "circle of animals," another name for zodiacal influences is "the beast." The purpose of initiation is to learn to master or control this "inner beast." So the Quran says of Joseph:

Oh my father, I saw eleven planets and the Sun and
the Moon. I saw them prostrating themselves to me.

-- Quran 12:4

The purpose of initiation is to make the entire zodiac -- as reflected in the body-mind-spirit complex -- submit to the higher nature or divine nature that's within man.

Joseph represented one planet and his brothers eleven more. This is an indication that at one time, the solar system was comprised of twelve planets which ruled the 12 signs. For more information, see my "Why Does Muhammad and Any Muslim Murder the Devil?" Yusuf represents the Sufic wisdom that enables one to master the zodiac.

Each of the twelve signs falls under one of four elements. There are actually five elements, but Western spiritual systems are generally limited to four: Earth, Air, Fire and Water. Earth signs (Taurus, Virgo and Capricorn) are considered practical and materialistic. Air signs (Gemini, Aquarius and Libra) are considered to be intellectual. Water signs (Cancer, Scorpio and Pisces) are considered to be emotional and Fire signs (Aries, Leo and Sagittarius) are considered to be passionate and energetic.

In Chinese astrology, Air is called Metal and Spirit (the 5th sign) is called Wood.

Published by: Fatir Publishing Text is copyright © 2014 Amir Fatir

Master Mantak Chia wrote: "The Taoists observed that Yin and Yang interactions universally follow five basic patterns, which came to be known as the Five Processes of Energy (or Five Phases or Five Forces). Such interactions have been erroneously translated as five elements, thereby confusing the process with the actual physical elements. In Taoism the physical elements found in nature symbolically express the motion of the Five Processes of Energy. Thus fire represents energy rising; water represents energy sinking; wood represents energy expanding; metal represents energy solidifying; and earth represents stable or centered energy. Each of the Five Processes of Energy depends on the interactions of Yin and Yang emanating from the primordial void." (Awaken Healing Light of the Tao).

The five elements are embedded secretly in the "five solar salaat" prayers that Muslims are to make each day.

Fajr (dawn) accords with fire (energy rising)
Dhur (noon) accords with wood (energy expanding)
'Asr (afternoon) accords with metal (energy solidifying)
Maghrib (sunset) accords with water (energy sinking)
'Isha (night) accords with Earth (stable energy)

Islam is a scientific spiritual system that cannot be understood and mastered without an understanding of the wisdom systems that are spread around the world because the Quran is the book that is the summary of the revelations to all nations before Muhammad and is a message to all nations.

Prophet Muhammad said: "Seek knowledge even far away as China."

Kalimat Shahadat: Witness the Letters
The First Pillar of Islam

Laa ilaaha illa Allah

The Book of Revelation (Injiyl) teaches that no one was worthy to loosen the seven seals off the scripture except a Lamb who was slain from the foundations of the earth.

And I saw in the right hand of him that sat

Published by: Fatir Publishing Text is copyright © 2014 Amir Fatir

on the throne a book written within and on the
backside, sealed with seven seals.

-- Revelation 5:1

The "book" is the totality of all scriptures of all the world's religions. All
these books or scriptures are sealed.

What is meant by "sealed?" It means that they are deliberately written in
code language so that the wicked and the ignorant could not decipher
them until "the fullness of time."

The scriptures were never intended to be understood by "the average
Joe." They were and are sacred (secret) texts that only the initiates could
properly read after many years of training and testing. That is why
Prophet Muhammad, before his initiation into the ancient wisdom, told
the archangel Gabriel "I cannot read." It is a mistake to think that Prophet
Muhammad could not read simple language. His being an "ummi," i.e.,
unlettered, is metaphoric.

Muhammad ibn Abdullah had been an international businessman for
more than 15 years before he was anointed a prophet. He conducted
business in Syria, Babylon, Jerusalem, Egypt, Ethiopia and other countries
on behalf of his wife, Khadijah. Is it realistic to believe that he conducted
large scale financial undertakings, including negotiating contracts and
long-term transactions, without being able to read and write the very
contracts he negotiated?

The above verse of Revelation says the book (i.e., the full library of
revealed scriptures) was written "within and on the backside."

That is saying that there is an inner meaning, a secret interpretation of
the scriptures as well as a misleading meaning for lay people who stumble
upon the writings without proper training.

The common understanding the world possesses of the Quran, Bible,
Upanishads, Vedas, Bhaga Vad Gita, Egyptian Pert em Hru and all other
books is the "backside" misunderstanding.

Published by: Fatir Publishing Text is copyright © 2014 Amir Fatir

There are seven levels of wisdom for each scriptural book. These seven levels are governed by seven spirits or seven planetary powers. In other words, there are seven levels of codes or "seven seals."

And I saw a strong angel proclaiming with a loud voice,
Who is worthy to open a book, and to loose the seven
seals thereof?

-- Revelation 5:2

The "I" of the above verse is actually Paul, writing under the alias "John." Paul was historically known as Apollonius of Tyana. A hint of this is provided in Acts where it states that Paul was called Apollo.

Apollo was Paul's Roman name and it means "Sun." Paul is a shortened form of Apollo. One of Paul's earlier names was "Saul." Saul means "Sol," another name of the Sun.

Paul traveled to India where he discovered and rewrote "The Initiation of the Anointed Iesous," a yoga scroll that depicted the kundalini initiation of Jesus Christ when he was mastering kundalini yoga. At that time, in that place, Jesus was known as Krishna ("our Christ"). That scroll became later called the Apocalypse and is currently titled Revelation.

The formally educated, the theologians and "mainstream" rabbis, imams, ministers and reverends are not worthy to open the book (the library of spiritual science texts).

"Opening the book" means to make its inner wisdom public. The mainstream theologians lack the knowledge to remove the codes that serve to seal the scriptures.

We may properly wonder why such eminent men and women are deemed unworthy? Unfortunately, in learning to become theologians, they were caught up in a Catch-22. The very education and indoctrination they underwent acted as a kind of brainwashing so that they have brought into the "backside" a red herring meaning of the scriptures. Their minds are locked into the camouflage. The few who are initiated in one of the secret orders cannot reveal what they've learned because they had to

Published by: Fatir Publishing Text is copyright © 2014 Amir Fatir

take a vow of silence (a vow to keep the secret (sacred) understanding from the "profane," i.e., the masses).

Added to that sorry state of affairs is the reality that established theologians in the mainstream of "Religion, Inc." are "bought and paid for" by the church, synagogue or mosque corporation under whose auspices they operate. Were they to espouse publicly anything other than "the party line," they would suddenly find themselves unemployed and at risk of losing the comfortable lifestyles provided clergymen and scholars who know how to behave themselves.

Consequently, the unfortunate theologians, esteemed though they may be, are considered unworthy to open the book or to remove the codes (seals) from it.

And no man in heaven, nor in earth,
neither under the earth, was able to
open the book, neither to look thereon.

-- Revelation 5:3

"Man," in the above verse, means mainstream scholar. Neither those in religion ("heaven"), in public ministries ("earth") or even in the secret societies ("under the earth") is able to open (publicize) the book or even acknowledge the truth that's contained ("look thereon") within it.

And I wept much, because no man
was found worthy to open and to read
the book, neither to look thereon.

-- Revelation 5:4

The mass insanity, schizophrenia, dissatisfied, grieved, angered, violent and self-destructive condition human society has plagued itself with is a result of the inability of "men" to properly decode the healing wisdom in the scripture. And if they cannot decode it, then it is impossible to correctly apply it. It is this sorrowful state of the world that is meant by the passage, "I wept much" in the verse quoted above.

And one of the elders saith unto me,

Published by: Fatir Publishing Text is copyright © 2014 Amir Fatir

Weep not: behold, the Lion of the
tribe of Juda, the Root of David, hath
prevailed to open the book, and to
loose the seven seals thereof.

-- Revelation 5:5

The Lion of Juda symbolizes one who has mastered the solar force which lies in the root chakra, the muladhara, and is able to activate it using pleasure-based (tantric) life force intensification procedures.

The Lion is a symbol of Leo and Leo is ruled by the Sun. David, which means "beloved," symbolizes here the male pleasure principle redirected from the root chakra (energy field) up the spinal canal.

And I beheld, and, lo, in the midst
of the throne and of the four beasts,
and in the midst of the elders, stood
a Lamb as it had been slain, having
seven horns and seven eyes, which
are the seven Spirits sent forth into
all the earth.

-- Revelation 5:6

The one worthy to open the book would receive his wisdom not from formal training in a theological cemetery (I mean seminary), but via meditation. The throne is a symbol of meditation. This symbol came from ancient Egypt where the goddess Isis (Auset) was the symbol of meditative trance. "Auset" means seat or throne. In Qaballah wisdom, trance meditation is called "Yesod" (seat or foundation).

The four beasts are Taurus, Scorpio, Leo and Aquarius. For a complete explanation of the four beasts, order my book Why Does Muhammad & Any Muslim Murder the Devil? It is available for $4.95 from UB & US Communications Systems, Inc. 912 W. Pembroke Ave., Hampton, VA 23669.

The symbol for Amen, in Egypt, was a Ram on a sacrificial alter. Later, just the alter was used.

Published by: Fatir Publishing Text is copyright © 2014 Amir Fatir

The Ram symbolized the sexual function, especially the urge to ejaculate. "Sacrificing" the Ram was a metaphor for sublimating the sexual creative urge and, via many procedures, raising it to a very high level.

So the Aries/Mars ejaculatory urge was "slain" and then "reborn" and thus a person attained the Amen level of hetep (peace) and power.

Some Egyptian icons showed the Lamb on the cross. This was later transferred to Christians who displayed Jesus on the cross and nicknamed him "the Lamb of God."

Mastery of the sexual function qualifies one to "read the Book."

And his brightness was as the
light; he had horns coming out
of his hand: and there was the
hiding of his power.

-- Habakkuk 3:4

This Lamb would hide his awesome power. The "horns" or forces in his hands represents the ability to activate the acupuncture chakra centers in the hand and to cause corresponding energy responses in the physical planet itself.

Yet he hid his power so that mankind would have the opportunity to repent, not from fear, but out of a willingness, nay, an eagerness, to do the right thing.

The Lamb's seven eyes are his full mastery of the seven chakras. The seven horns are the sound vibrations (mantric words of power called a trumpet in other passages) which evoke the Shekinah (shakti) power.

These seven energies (spirits) go throughout the Lamb's entire body ("all the earth") so even if his physical hands are amputated, it is too late to negate his power.

And he came and took the book
out of the right hand of him that

Published by: Fatir Publishing Text is copyright © 2014 Amir Fatir

sat upon the throne.

-- Revelation 5:7

Notice that the Lamb didn't politely request the book. Rather he boldly stepped forward and took the book. This represents the seizure of power over the dissemination of the scientific religious wisdom.

The Holy Quran is a summation, in a condensed form, of the wisdom contained in all previous scriptures. It is not an Arab book or a "black" book or a "white" book, nor is it a book that's simply for people who call themselves Muslims. The Quran is "a message to all nations" and is equally for white people, black people, Chinese people, Indian people, Jewish people, Sabian people, Buddhist people, Hindu people and Christian people.

However, the Quran, like the full library of revelation, is not correctly interpreted by mainstream scholars.

The Quran is the scriptural revelation given to Prophet Muhammad by the archangel Gabriel. However, it was not written by Gabriel, it was revealed by Gabriel. Does this actually mean that a ghostly figure brought the Quran to Muhammad chapter after chapter?

In former times such a Sunday school understanding of the wisdom tradition may have been adequate. However, in the face of the horrible condition of the world and the disunity among peoples, a "unified field" understanding of scripture is necessary if we are to survive.

Gabriel is the archangel of the 9th Sphere of the Tree of Life, Yesod. In saying that Gabriel brought down the revelation, the Quran is indicating that the revelation was made possible because of Muhammad's remarkable ability to induce trance.

Say: Whoever became an enemy to
Gabriel -- for surely he brought it
down to him upon your heart by the
permission of Allah, a confirmation of
what is between your hand (i.e in front
of you) and a guidance to the believers.

-- Quran 2:97

Meditation "expands thy breast" so that the meditator is able to receive the Book of Allah on his heart (i.e., according to his moral capacity).

But if Muhammad didn't write the Quran and if Gabriel is not the author of it, then who wrote the Quran?

A much maligned Lesson of the Nation of Islam asks:

Who made the Holy Quran or Bible, how long ago?

Answer: The original people who is Allah, the supreme being or black man of Asia.

More than a few Muslims scoff at the Honorable Elijah Muhammad's explanation of the authorship of the Quran. I humbly ask them to look again and to try to look without prejudice.

Here is what the Quran itself says about the authorship of all the scriptures (including the Quran):

11. It is indeed a message of instruction.
12. Therefore let whoso will, keep it in remembrance.
13. (It is) in Books held (greatly) in honour.
14. Exalted (in dignity), kept pure and holy.
15. (Written) by the hands of scribes --
16. Remarkable and Pious and Just.

-- Quran 80:11-17
Yusuf Ali Translation

The Quran was "written by the hands of scribes." These "scribes" are not the ordinary human secretaries Muhammad employed to write down his trance channelled utterances for these books are "exalted," i.e., found on the heavenly spiritual planes. These scribes are higher beings.

The Honorable Elijah Muhammad was not teaching an understanding contrary to that of the Quran itself when he stated that the Quran was written by "the original people who is Allah, the supreme being or black man of Asia." The worst he can be criticized for is an improper use of the verb to be.

There are four Qaballistic worlds or planes (dimensions). To fully comprehend Elijah Muhammad's "mathematic theology" a working knowledge of the sacred (secret) wisdom would be invaluable.

The four worlds of the Qaballah are Assiah, Yetzirah, Briyah and Atziluth. "Asia," in Elijah Muhammad's theology, is code for the Qaballistic world Assiah.

Assiah starts at the physical universe and extends to the lower part of the Astral Plane. In essence, Elijah Muhammad was saying that Quranic writing descends to human consciousness from the spiritual realm. this accords with Prophet Muhammad's ascension to the heavenly planes during the Night Journey. At one point on the journey the Prophet reported of hearing the scratching of the pens of those who wrote the Book of Allah.

"Black man" is code for the deep state of mind where there is no movement of thought in the consciousness. The absence of movement is metaphorically "black" because without movement nothing, not even light, can propogate. The mind here comes to rest, the stillness that is the goal of meditation is achieved. This is the state of consciousness that yogis refer to as Samadhi.

O soul that is at rest!
Return to your Lord,
well pleased, well pleasing.
So enter through My slaves.
And enter My garden.

-- Quran 89:27-30

Samadhi is also mentioned in the famous "Ikhlaas" chapter:

Say: He is Allah Unified
Allah is the Samad [i.e., the
Undifferentiated state of Being].

Published by: Fatir Publishing Text is copyright © 2014 Amir Fatir

It never reproduced (Itself) and
It was never reproduced.
And nothing could ever become
an equal to It.

-- Quran 112:1-4

The Arabic "Samad" is the same technical word as the yogic "Samadhi."
When the meditator achieves this superconscious state the supreme life
force (Allah) is unified and he recognizes or realizes that one life
permeates all that is. This consciousness is of everything for everything is
an expression of the One. Nothing but Itself exists, it never reproduced
and it cannot be reproduced because it is All That Is.

It is important for students of the Quran to learn to read it in Arabic
because significant passages of the existing popular English translations
are incorrectly translated.

Without a correct understanding of some very technical terms, the very
root and foundation of the world's understanding of al-Islam will remain
flawed.

With all due respect, I must make it clear that the very core understanding
extant about Islamic principles is incorrect. Even the five pillars of Islam
are inadequately and improperly understood.

The kalimat shahadat is more than a simple declaration of faith.

Salaat is more than just a prayer.

Zakaat is more than just charity.

Siyaam is more than mere fasting during Ramadan or at any other time.

Hajj means more than pilgrimage to Mecca or any other holy city.

And when Abraham and Ishmael
raised the foundations of the House.

-- Quran 2:127

Published by: Fatir Publishing Text is copyright © 2014 Amir Fatir

The very foundation of the understanding of al-Islam is in need of repair even as Father Abraham and Ishmael repaired the House and raised its foundations.

We are engaged in repairing the House of Islam, raising its very foundations. The time has come for the faith to be revived and renewed.

The former system simply does not work! How can I make such a statement? Well, the Quran says that Muhammad is the pattern for the believers to form themselves after. If the system as we presently possess it worked, there would be many, many people just like Muhammad. Islam has been taught as an organized religion for over 1500 years. There are currently one billion Muslims alive in the world and many more billions who have died. Yet in all those billions, Islam has failed to produce a single Muhammad since the death of Prophet Muhammad.

That is why I can make the statement that the system doesn't work. Bring me 10 Muhammads. Bring me five. Bring me one man who is equal to Muhammad and I will stop and say "Islam works." But if you cannot, then please recognize that we must do our best, by Allah's permission, to raise the foundations of the house.

Allah! There is no god But He -- the Living, the
Self-subsisting, Eternal. No slumber can seize
Him nor sleep. His are all things in the heavens
and on earth. Who is there can intercede in His
presence except as he permitteth?
He knoweth what (appeareth to His creatures as)
Before or After or behind them.
Nor shall they compass aught of His knowledge
except as He willeth.
His Throne doth extend over the heavens
and the earth, and He feeleth no fatigue in
guarding and preserving them for He is
the Most High, the Supreme (in glory).

-- Quran 2:255 Yusuf Ali Translation

Published by: Fatir Publishing Text is copyright © 2014 Amir Fatir

The esteemed scholar Yusuf Ali translated the first part of the above verse: "Allah! There is no god but He." This is translated from the Arabic words, "Allah laa ilaaha illa huwa." This is slightly modified in the kalimat shahadat (public testimony) as it is currently understood: "Laa ilaaha illa Allah," which is translated "There is no god but Allah."

This statement forms perhaps the most important statement in all of Islam. Yet even this statement is understood and translated incorrectly.

And ye shall know the truth, and
the truth shall make you free.

-- John 8:32

Arabic nouns end with a tanwin. Depending upon whether the statement is in the genitive, nominative or accusative case, the tanwin is transliterated "in," "un," or "an." That is illustrated in such statements as "Muhammad-an Rasulullah."

If the word ilaaha was to be translated "god" then it would have to be a noun and it would also have to have a tanwin suffix.

You must learn to use the language in
its proper terms in order to gain some
benefit for self.

-- Master Fard Muhammad

"Ilaaha" is not a noun in Quran 2:255, it's a verb. As such, the sentence cannot be properly translated "there is not god but He" because god is a noun and ilaaha lacks a tanwin.

The correct translation is "Allah! Nothing deifies except He."

This corrected translation suddenly gives us a horse of an entirely different color.

Jesus taught that "Ye are all gods, children of the most high." The depth science of all scripture is that man can potentially become a "true and living god." The Sufis indicated the same when they would declare, "Ana-

1-haqq," which means "I am the Truth." (Haqq is one of the 99 Names of Allah).

For declaring this truth many Sufis were murdered by those who didn't understand.

There came to you Messengers
before me, with Clear Signs and even
with what ye ask for: why then did ye
slay them, if ye speak the truth?

-- Quran 3:183

Many are the messengers of the Lord who are crucified by fanatics who, out of ignorance, think they are justified in killing righteous women and men.

Father, forgive them; for they
know not what they do.

-- Luke 23:34

For teaching that "I and the Father are one" and that "ye are all gods," Jesus was stoned.

Why is this knowledge so upsetting? Why do ignorant men reject it out of hand without investigation or even attempt to experience what would be the greatest blessing a human could receive? Why is the revelation of the potential of humanity not a cause for rejoicing?

When human beings are confronted with the reality of their divine potential, they are forced to stop blaming their misfortunes upon others. There is something fundamentally flawed in humanity that causes us to wish to place blame on others. Even in the Genesis myth, Adam didn't own up to his disobedience is eating from the tree of good and evil. Rather, when confronted with his disobedience, he said, "The woman you gave me told me to eat it."

Most of us would rather blame others instead of realizing that we have the full potential to create our personal universe as we will. In fact, the universe in which we live is a reflection of our own beliefs, ideas, feelings, emotions, aspirations and thoughts.

The masses are afraid of the responsibility (the ability to respond) which potential divinity awakens them to and the ruling bodies fear that people who realize their inner divinity will cease to allow them to exploit and oppress them for their own ego gratification.

The revelation that "ye are all gods" forces us to get up and do something for ourselves. Most people would prefer to sacrifice their birthright for the false comfort of being "taken care of" by some tyrant who is usually just as ignorant as the people he oppresses.

"Laa ilaaha illa Huwa." Who is Huwa? Huwa (also called Hu, Hua, Hum and Hung) is the great divine intelligence known to the ancient Egyptians as Tehuti. Some esoteric Jews refer to Him as "O He!"

The divine intelligence deifies, it transforms animalistic man into divine man. Huwa turns "sinful flesh" into flesh divine.

The first pillar of Islam is Kalimat Shahadat. Until now, Kalimat Shahadat has been explained as "openly bearing witness that there is no God but Allah."

The Arabic word "Kalimat" means "Letters." The Arabic word "Shahadat" means "Witness."

Then Adam learned Letters from his Lord.

-- Quaran 2:31

Kalimat Shahadat means to "Witness the Letters." But what are the Letters that initiates are supposed to witness and what does it mean to witness?

There is witness by sense of feeling, by hearing and by sight. As the Quran says, "Ye shall see it with certainty of sight" ('ayn al-yaqin).

The Letters that initiates must witness are the 14 Mystic Letters (al-Mugatta'aat) that open 29 Surahs of the Quran. Each Letter represents a sound vibration that's called a bija (seed mantra) in yoga. These sounds are the 14 root sounds which represent the primary aspects of the solar force that the ancient Egyptians called the 14 Kau (Transformations) of Ra. They are expressed in the earth and in the body as seven planetary powers which have two main modes: attraction and repulsion.

The initiate learns to feel the energies represented by these sounds. Later she learns to hear them. At a later stage of development she learns to see them "with certainty of sight." It is only at this point that she can truly express the Kalimat Shahadat and here that she has fulfilled the first pillar of al-Islam.

The 14 Letters are imbedded in chakras (energy centers) located beneath the skin on the 14 finger segments of your right hand. For example, upon the index finger are the Letters Alif Laam and Mim (A.L.M.) and when the Muslim raises his finger in greeting, he is actually saying, "Alif Laam Mim, I have mastered these Letters and can now read the Book of Allah (the Akashic Record)."

Salaat: The Kundalini Yoga of Islam

Kundalini yoga is the yoga that focuses upon activating energy that resides in the base of the spine. The kundalini yogi lifts that energy by various techniques from the lowest chakra (energy center) up to the highest chakra.

There are many chakras in the body, but most kundalini teachers focus on 7 of them which are along the spinal column. The chakras are named as follows and located as indicated:

NAME	LOCATION	PLANET	VIRTUE
Muladhara	Above anus	Mars	Survival, self-defense
Svadhishthana	Genitals	Moon	Sensuality, Sex
Manipura	Solar Plexus	Mercury	Power, ego
Anahata	Heart	Sun	Love, compassion
Vishuddha	Throat	Venus	Devotion, creativity
Ajna	Forehead	Jupiter	Wisdom, self-realization

Sahasrara	Crown of Head	Saturn	Enlightenment

In addition to the 7 chakras, in the kundalini system, there are three pathways called nadis which are subtler than nerves. They are more like the acupuncture meridians through which Chi flows. But if acupuncture meridians are likened to roads, the three nadis are superhighways. They are named the Ida, Pingala and Sushumna.

The Ida nadi begins at the left nostril, goes to the left cerebral cortex region of the brain, crosses over, now moving downward, to the middle of the forehead, between the eyebrows and just above them.

The Pingala nadi begins at the right nostril and goes up to the right cerebral cortex and goes down to crisscross the Ida at the forehead.

These nadis crisscross each other descending the spinal cord and the places at which they intersect are the chakras. Chakras are spoken of in the Bible as Ezekiel's wheels as the word chakra means "wheel."

The main nadi is inside the spinal cord. It is the sushumna nadi. By special breathing techniques (pranayama) or by concentration or by employing mantras, the energy that's at the base of the spine, coiled up like a serpent, is made to rise out of its slumber and break through the chakra centers along the spine. At the chakra center is pierced by the "serpentine fire" of kundalini, various abilities are said to unfold for the yogi.

The kundalini energy (shakti) at the base of the spine is called "solar force," "libido," "serpent power," "serpentine fire." There are many who believe that the hidden theme of Western religious scripture is the kundalini and its elevation.

The ancient Egyptians called kundalini power "Ra, who is symbolized as the sun because the sun is the source of the kundalini force.

In Al-Islam, kundalini power is known as salaat.

Have you considered Al-Lat, Al-'Uzza and Manat,
the third, the other? Are the males for you and
for him the females?

Published by: Fatir Publishing Text is copyright © 2014 Amir Fatir

-- Quran 53: 19-21

The ancient Arabs believed that Allah had a counterpart and Her name as Al-Lat. It is common among the religions of antiquity for the God to have a wife or consort. This represents the compliment or opposite polarity of the energy of which the God Himself was a symbol.

It should be pointed out here that as Islam gives Allah 99 attributes, so do other religions give attributes to the One God of their faith. These deities are not separate any more than Allah is considered to share His Kingdom with 99 other deities like As-Salaam, An-Nur or Al-Wadud. The 99 names are 99 expressions of the one supreme being.

The Egyptian religion is the root of the three western religions' concepts. In the Egyptian religion, each major divine attribute was metamorphized into a deity. The consciousness of the God Amen was said to be another god, Sa. Sa was always paired with the god Hu.

The Arabic word "salaat" is comprised a "sa" and "laat" (from Al-Laat, the wife of Allah in primitive Arabic theology).

As kundalini is regarded as the feminine expression of the divine force, and as Mother Rat is the wife of Ra in Egyptian theology, Allat is the feminine force shakt: that forms the active energy of kundalini and is matched with "Sa" or consciousness and now comes down to us as the solar based prayer system called "sa-laat."

"Manat" corresponds to Venus and the Egyptian goddess of the planet Venus, Het-Heru, it is in charge of storing the sexual Ra or kundalini force (known in Freudian psychoanalysis as "libido").

Salaat is regulated by the five positions of the sun. In yoga there is a very similar exercise of movements that is known as the Sun Salutation. So on one hand we have "sun salute" (yoga) and on the other solar regulated salaat. The similarity of the words and the movements should indicate to even the dimmest most dogmatic religious mind that the two things are at the very least related.

The Egyptian religion features Heru and his four sons. As Heru is symbolized by the sun (Heru is nearly identical to Ra -- but Heru represents the focus of consciousness while Ra represents the subconscious), his four sons represent four modalities of the solar force.

The same four modalities are incorporated in the solar regulated salaat times of al-Islam. Heru is represented by the Noon Sun, the Sun when it is at its highest and brightest.

Fajr, 'Asr, Maghrib and 'Isha are Islamic correlates to the four sons of Heru. Together with Dhur (noon), they represent the five time periods when the solar current is active according to the element the particular solar current is conveying.

The word "salaat" means "burning fire." This corresponds to the meaning of kundalini as "serpentine fire."

We have made the salaat a
book of time.

-- Quran

Salaat as a book of time refers to the time to activate the solar force in the spine according to the element that's operating.

The salaat as a Book of time also refers to the entire Injil or Book of Revelation, the scripture given to Jesus. This Book's entire subject is the raising of the kundalini.

The yoga sun salute features postures (asanas) that are similar to those of Muslim solar salaat positions.

In Qiyaam the Muslim stands erect with his hands cupped together as he begins a supplication (dua). The yogi stands erect as he begins his sun salute with his hands pointed up, palms together, in the "namaste" pose Christians use for prayer. Before each movement, the Muslim raises his hands to his ears and says "allau akbar." The Yogi raises his hands all the way back.

In Ruku' the Muslim bends forward with his hands on his knees. The yogi bends all the way forward, touches the floor or his toes with his hands and then presses his head to his knees. The benefit of this posture is that it opens the spinal cord, loosening it, making it more elastic. It is said that a person's body is as old as his spinal cord is stiff. The forward bend (ruku') allows the Muslim to open the chakras along his spine. It accomplishes the same for the yogi.

Qiyaam establishes correct posture. It is called, in yoga, the Tree Pose. This is related to the fact that Ausar (God in Egyptian religion) was buried in a tree. This posture (qiyaam) aligns the vertebrae along the spinal cord. It also permits the relaxation response to begin.

Both the yogi and the Muslim make prostration. This posture (sajda in Islam) allows for blood to flow to the brain, thus enriching the pineal and pituitary glands (which operate along with the sahsrara and ajna chakras, respectively).

The enriched blood flow to the brain makes it easier for the Muslim to experience al-bayyinat (clear visions) and prepare the brain for the awesome kundalini (salaat) energy when it rises to the two highest chakras.

The additional blood centered in the brain also helps to provide moisture for the brain so that it doesn't overheat when the salaat (kundalini) fire rises up to the brain centers. This helps to prevent such things as kundalini psychosis and fevers. The Muslim version of sajdah is quite a bit like the headstand in terms of physiological effects.

The Muslim goes into jalsa (the short sitting pose) while the yogi goes into a kind of backwards bend that's called the downward facing dog. In that pose, the yogi's buttocks is raised in the air while he is supported on his hands and feet. Stretching is accomplished in the hamstring and calve muscles. This stretching eliminates some pranic waste from the meridians (nadis) so that fresh spirit energy can be brought inside the body.

For the Muslim, jalsa enables him to activate the nadi (acupuncture meridian) in the right big toe. There are two organs of the body which are affected by this point, the liver and the spleen. Proper performance of jalsa may have a beneficial effect upon the health of the liver and spleen.

Following completion of the asanas of the yogic sun salute, the yogi goes into the corpse pose wherein he lies on his back to meditate.

Call on Allah whether standing, sitting or lying
on your side

-- Quran

The Muslim, on the other hand, goes into qada'ah or the long sitting pose. In proper performance of qada'ah, the Muslim sits down on his bottom and crosses his legs and then performs meditation, especially the meditation of dhikr (chanting the names of Allah and/or the Mystic Letters).

It is in the position of qada'ah that salaat proper actually occurs for it is here, owing to the use of dhikr and pranayama, that the salaat force is actually lifted up from the base of the spine.

Properly translated from the Arabic, the Quaranic injunction is not to perform prayer, but to "raise up the salaat." This is identical to the yogic effort to raise up the kundalini.

In qada'ah the Muslim performs the necessary chantings and breathings to raise up the fire of Allah or the serpentine fire.

This is often accomplished by special breathing alternately from the right to the left nostril and vice-versa. This is called nadi sodhana breathing. Use of both these nadis starts a positive and negative polarity to occur along the spinal cord (sushumna nadi) and eventually the inner fire ignites and lifts up along the spine.

Because this process may take hours, the Quran tells the Muslim to perform salaat from, for example, the beginning of 'Asr until the beginning of Maghrib. This could be hours of salaat performance and, especially early in initiation, raising the kundalini (salaat) may indeed take that long. For some it may take much longer, and to be perfectly frank, there is little probability of anyone raising it the first attempt that is made. A certain degree of dedication and perseverance is required.

The seat in qada'ah grounds the muladhara chakra to the ground and that helps prevent an overabundance of salaat force from rushing through the body, potentially causing harm. the connection with the earth facilitates healing and the maintenance of good health.

Wudu cools the body by applying water to the places most likely to overheat when the salaat force is raised. The Muslim cools his head, his hands, his arms, his feet, his ears and neck. He washes his mouth out and he cleanses his nostrils by sniffing water up his nostrils before performing the salaat raising.

Tayammun is an Islamic ablution practice of using clean earth to prepare for prayer when water is not available. Tayammun, connecting the Muslim again to Mother Earth, helps to ground him so his body is not shocked by the awesome salaat force when it wakes up. It also makes for a good environment for bodily healing.

The sniffing of water up the nostrils brings the Ida and Pingala nadis into activation.

Surely the raising by night is the firmest for
speech.

-- Quran 73:6

The improvement upon speech is actually meant the making of words of power effective and potent. When that happens, i.e., when a Muslim's mantras are powerfully pronounced to bring about a true effect, that Muslim is then considered to be "As-Saddiyq," the true of speech. In Egyptian theology, he is called "maa kheru," i.e., "true of speech." By raising up at night to perform these mantras, they are nearer to the deepest Collective Subconscious ("the deity Ausar") where the power lies to bring them into manifestation.

The goals of salaat include astral travelling ("night journey," according to Quranic terminology); spiritual purification, and entering the heavenly state of consciousness and being.

Oh thou soul that art at rest.
come back thou to thy Lord, well pleased

and well pleasing.
Enter then among my devotees.
Yeah, enter thou my garden.

-- Holy Quran 89:27-30

The medical staff with two serpents entwining a staff is a symbol of kundalini. The two serpents represent the Ida and Pingala nadis.

The wings at the top symbolize the flight the initiate can take after the kundalini force is lifted to the sahasrara chakra. This flight symbolizes astral projection.

Even in the performance of traditional salaat, the Muslim will often feel his temperature increase. This is the purification process that salaat even incompletely performed, makes happen.

Salaat is kundalini and kundalini is salaat. A complete study of the yogic kundalini system is required in order for us to fulfil the second pillar of the faith.

Salaat should not be confused with dua. The latter is more in accord with the idea of "prayer."

The ancients recognized that the flame that runs from the base of the spine to the top of the head is almost always stuck in the lower spine, at the muladhara chakra which is near the anus. Serious effort is required to lift that flame from the lower spine up through the various chakras to either the forehead or the crown of the head. The higher the initiate is able to raise the salaat flame, the more powers he is able to gain.

When the Muslim yogi reads of Ra, Ra-t, kundalini, chi, orgone or libido, she is reading of salaat. The early Nazarenes saw that the salaat force was interrelated with the solar (Sun) force and named that force Samson (Shams-an). Samson means "Sun."

"Hayya 'alay salaat," in the Adhan (Call to Prayer) should be understood as meaning: "Life (hayya) is dependent upon ('alay) kundalini (salaat)."

Which means that spiritual life requires the raising up of the kundalini force and life is upon or with (as gas is an integral part of oil) kundalini.

To symbolize the ascension of the salaat to the higher chakras, the yogis of India placed a dot on their forehead. The Christians place ashes on their forehead on Ash Wednesday. The ancient Egyptians wore a tiara (headband) with a small serpent sticking out (the serpentine fire rising out of the pituitary gland). The Muslims have a prostration mark which is actually a symbol of the lifting up of the solar power to the forehead.

Many monks shaved the center of the top of their heads, the crown, to symbolize that they have raised the kundalini power to their crown chakras.

The meaning of these symbols has been lost upon many and few orders actually practice kundalini raising today. But that is the root of the above symbolic dress and adornments.

There are said to be dangers connected with raising up the salaat without appropriate training. Those dangers include such things a kundalini psychosis, sexual obsession, overheating of the body felt in the head and heart and even spontaneous combustion.

I do not personally know of anyone who has experienced such side-effects from kundalini. Taoist yoga advises an initiate to ground the energy and circulate the salaat force in a cycle around the entire body. The kundalini focus on the spine is the primary Indian yoga approach while the Chinese yoga approach is based upon grounding and the Microcosmic Orbit.

It should be pointed out here that "Tao" is derived from the Coptic Egyptian name for Tehuti, "Taout."

The teaching of kundalini yoga through direct raising of the energy up the spine to the crown is considered dangerous.

The primary variance between the priests of Ra of ancient Egypt and the priests of Osiris relates to this same difference in the treatment of the kundalini force.

Zakaat: The Third Pillar of Islam

The true meaning of zakaat is purification. Zakaat, however, has been erroneously defined as "charity" and "poor tax."

Zakaat encompasses and entire range of physical, moral and mental purification rituals that includes yogic breathing, enemas, colonics, cleaning the tongue, clearing the acupuncture meridians, cleaning the stomach and cleaning the mind of dirty thoughts (samskaras).

Purification (zakaat) strengthens the experience of salaat (kundalini activation) because cleansed nerves and nadis (meridians) allows the chi (salaat) force to flow more freely and more potently.

And raise up the salaat [kundalini]
and bring the purification [zakaat].
And whatever you send forward for your
souls of good you find it with Allah.
Surely Allah is a Seer of what you do.

-- Quran 2:110

Giving another a massage is a form of "giving the zakaat" because massage clears the body tissue and organs (as well as the nadis) of collected obstructions and filth. In Christian scriptures massage is called "the laying on of hands." The energy in the chakra centers in the hands serves to move into the body of the person receiving the massage so that she experiences the activation of her own cleansing energies. Massage is best conducted by someone of another sex because the opposite polarity of energy better calls the other person's chi energy into activation.

When you read in the New Testament of so much foot washing, you are reading of the use of massage of various acupuncture points in the foot, big toe and ankles.

The acupuncture point in the sole of the foot is called Yong-Quan (Bubbling Spring). Massage of this point opens the way for the energy of the Earth to flow inside the body and promote healing. Sick energy can also be passed out of the body through this point to be recycled by Mother Earth.

The acupuncture point below the ankle is called Chao Hai, the Shining Sea. It aids the health of the kidneys.

The acupuncture point inside the bottom of the foot, in the hollow behind the third joint of the big toe is called Kung Sun, the Grandson. It promotes the health of the spleen.

The acupuncture point on the top and outside of the foot where the joint between the fourth and little toes is located is called Lin Chi, Attending the Crying Child. It promotes the health of the gall bladder.

The acupuncture point on the outside of the ankle in the small depression under and slightly between the ankle bone is called Shenmai, Extending Vessel. It promotes the health of the bladder.

Da Dun is the name of the point on the inside of the big toe at the corner of the toenail and the joint. Massage of this point helps cleanse and harmonize spiritual energy passing through it.

The Earth contains purifying and healing energies and that is why Muslims are to remove their shoes before prayer and during visits to the mosque.

Zakaat also means "increase" because a purified body/mind is free to expand. The result of zakaat (purification) is less waste of resources on meat, medicine, drugs, alcohol, tobacco, extracurricular sex, sport and play. So the master of zakaat will find that she or he has increased his or her wealth by not spending it foolishly. She is therefore in an improved position to give charity. Thus, the giving of charity is the effect of zakaat, not zakaat itself.

Fasting is a kind of zakaat because fasting clears the colon and cleans the blood.

Siyaam: The Fourth Pillar of Islam

Saum or Siyaam is the fourth pillar of al-Islam.

O you who believe!
Siyaam is written upon you

Published by: Fatir Publishing Text is copyright © 2014 Amir Fatir

just like it was written upon
those who were before you that
you might realize God.

-- Quran 2:183

Siyaam is usually translated "fasting." However, there are different kinds
of fasts. Mary, for example, and Zakariyya were placed on fasts of silence.

He [Zakariyya] said: "My Lord, make
a sign for me. He said, your sign will
be that you do not speak to the people
for three nights straight.

-- Quran 19:10

So eat and drink and cool (your) eye.
And if you see any man, say, "I have vowed
a saum [translated "fast"] to Al-Rahman,
so I will not speak to a man today."

-- Quran 19:26

In Mary's "fast," she is told to both eat and drink. Even if this was in fact a
fast of silence, she is also told to speak. Mary's situation can be
understood more properly with a little background.

Mary was in India at the time of this instruction and that is why she says
she had vowed a saum to Al-Rahman. Al-Rahman is the Arabic equivalent
of Brahman, the Supreme Deity of the people of ancient India.

If Mary's so-called fast permitted her to eat, drink and even to speak, then
what type of "fast" was the virgin on?

Mary's saum was for abstaining from sexual intercourse.

And Mary the daughter of 'Imran, who guarded
her vagina [farjahaa]. So we breathed into
it [her vagina] Our Spirit and she spoke
truthfully with the Words of her Lord and

His Scriptures. And she had been one of
celibate ones.

-- Quran 66:12

Mary was dedicated as a special vessel to God from before her birth. Her
mother had been so dedicated before Mary's own birth and no man was
to have sexual intercourse with Mary. Her encounter was to be with the
Spirit and so the Quran says "We blew Our Spirit into it."

Mary had gone to "a place in the East," i.e., India. There she underwent
initiation for she was, herself, a prophetess. This is shown in the old
testament where Merriam (same as Maryam) is addressed as "O sister of
Aaron" (as she is also addressed in the Quran) and, like the Quranic and
New Testament Mary, she is the daughter of Amran ('Imran). The Old
Testament Merriam is the same person as the Quranic Maryam. She was
the sister of Moses and Aaron and a prophetess. Mary, the mother of
Jesus, is the young lady who pulled Moses out of the Nile river and
presented him to Pharaoh's wife as an adopted son.

The New Testament myth of her being "betroathed to Joseph" is code
language. Joseph is Yusuf in Arabic and Yusuf symbolizes Sufic wisdom,
especially wisdom from the dream world. She was an initiate in the
wisdom of the Sufis, not betroathed (engaged) in the ordinary sense of
the word.

When Mary was studying in India marauding males thought little of
attacking and raping a woman who was unprotected. The few women
who were generally free from such abuse were those who were celibate
for the sake of Brahman. So in her travels in that country she was told that
if a man approached her to tell him that she belonged to Brahman. His
own fear of Brahman would protect her from rape.

This was the atmosphere of which the Quran relates in these words:

She took from beneath them a veil
(to veil herself) from them. Then
We sent to her Our Spirit, and he
appeared to her as a perfect man.

She said: "I seek refuge from you
to Al-Rahman, if you are afraid
(of Brahman)."

He said: "Surely what I am is a
Messenger of your Lord to give
you a pure boy."

She said: "How can there be a
boy for me and never has a mortal
touched me and I have never been a whore."

He said: "Like that!" Your Lord said,
'For Me it is an easy thing. And to
make him a sign to humanity and a
mercy from Us.' And it had been
a predestined matter."

-- Quran 19:17-21

When had Mary's conception and delivery of Jesus become a
"predestined matter?"

The Quranic Surah 3 is entitled "The Family of Amran" ('Imran). 'Imran
was the father of Mary, Moses and Aaron.

Behold! a woman of 'Imran said: 'O my Lord!
I do dedicate unto thee what is in my womb for
Thy special service. So accept this of me: For
thou hearest and knoweth all things.

When she was delivered, she said: "Oh my Lord!
Behold! I am delivered of a female child!" And
Allah knew best what she brought forth -- "And no
wise is the male like the female. I have named her
Mary, and I commend her and her offspring to Thee
from Satan the Rejected.

With a beautiful acceptance (Mary was accepted). And
He grew (into) a beautiful growing.

Published by: Fatir Publishing Text is copyright © 2014 Amir Fatir

-- Quran 3:35-37

Hanna (or Anna), Mary's mother, became pregnant by her husband
Amran. She vowed her child to be Muharrar. A kind of monk would be the
closest well known modern similarity to a Muharrar. But instead of having
a son, she was shocked to learn that she bore a little baby girl. Still she
dedicated her baby girl to becoming the female equivalent of a male
Muharrar (which is rather similar to a modern nun). That is when Mary's
future motherhood of Jesus became "a predestined matter."

That is why Mary did not have sex with mortals before the birth of Christ
and that is why the men were so shocked when she came back from India
carrying a little baby boy (Jesus).

At length she brought the (babe) to her people,
carrying him (in her arms). They said, "O Mary!
Surely you have brought a strange thing."

-- Quran 19:27

It was strange because she was to remain a virgin and now, obviously
having had a baby, the theologians of her people were shocked.

"O sister of Aaron! Your father was not an
evil man and your mother was not a whore!"

-- Quran 19:28

In essence, the theologians were saying, "How could you do this? You
come from a good family. Where in the world did this whorish behavior of
yours come from?"

But she pointed to the baby.
They said: "How can we talk to one who a
child in the cradle?"

(The baby) said: "I am indeed a servant of
Allah: He has given me the Scripture and made
me a prophet.

Published by: Fatir Publishing Text is copyright © 2014 Amir Fatir

And He has made me blessed wheresoever I be, and has enjoined on me Salaat [kundalini raising] and Zakaat [purification rituals] as long as I live."

"And kind to my mother, and not overbearing or miserable."

-- Quran 19:29-32

Jesus came to the defense of his mother and obliquely warned them against harming her by saying "and kind to my mother." Being in possession of salaat ([kundalini shakti] faculties, he could have defended his mother against attack.

Fasting from food and drink can be an element of Siyaam, but such fasting is not Siyaam itself.

Siyaam actually means abstention from sex "for a fixed number of days." Fasting from food removes the concentration of blood from the lower part of the body, reduces the body fluid from seeping from the stomach into the genitals and thus makes it easier to abstain from sex.

Eating is intimately connected with sex. The lips are the first erogenous zone to become active in a child.

When a man seeks to seduce a woman, he often takes her to dinner. Food consumption produces the body and psychic environment for the activation of sexual desire.

Some people are caught in a vicious food-sex cycle. They eat and the body's blood floods the stomach area to process food. The fluids seep into the genital region, exciting them. The person then engages in sex and the expended energy (caloric burn up) from the sex gives them an appetite for food. After eating, they desire sleep or if they sleep first, they awaken with a feeling of renewed hunger. The satisfaction of the hunger generates another interest in a sexual encounter.

Fasting reduces the sexual need and for men allows them to retain the supply of seminal fluid necessary to awaken the Salaat (Kundalini) force.

An abundance of retained sexual energy is essential for Salaat activation. The proper observance of the 4th pillar of al-Islam (abstention from sex) reinforces the 2nd pillar (Salaat/Kundalini raising).

Sexual abstention is not to be a lifelong endeavour. It should be observed "for a fixed number of days."

The male initiate learns to engage in frequent sexual intercourse, if that is his desire, but can climax without releasing his semen. He is able to circulate the sexual force up his spine and down his front channel experiencing ecstasy ("the Garden of Bliss") in various body centers and even achieving a whole body orgasm.

Sexual initiation for women is equally important. A full discussion of women's sexual spirituality is provided in my book "Tantric Sex Magic Rituals for Modern Women."

Hajj: The Fifth Pillar of Islam

The fifth pillar of al-Islam is Hajj. Hajj means "conquest" and a hajji is a conqueror.

Proper observance of Pillars 2, 3 and 4 permits the Muslims to conquer his body and mind.

A hajji is a full initiate. This conquest opens the way for the Muslim to travel outside his body and thus he can be a pilgrim, traveling to spiritual dimensions, liberated of bodily captivity.

The pilgrimage to Mecca is a ritual that provides a sign of the inner hajj.

The Black Stone in the ka'aba symbolizes the return of Arabs home to kiss their black mother, Hagar (whose name means stone).

The seven orbits around the ka'aba symbolize the circulation of light ritual that Taoist yogis call the Small Heavenly Circle or the Microcosmic Orbit.

Published by: Fatir Publishing Text is copyright © 2014 Amir Fatir

Throwing seven stones at the white rock symbolizes a rejection of the incomplete seven chakra system of Indian kundalini yoga in favor of the more holistic yin/yang blending of the Small Heavenly Circle.

It is not permitted to the Sun to
catch up the Moon, nor can the
Night outstrip the Day: Each (just)
swims along in (its own) orbit.

-- Quran 36:40

The yin energy of the Functional Channel is considered to be related to the moon. The yang energy of the Governor Channel is considered to be related to the Sun. These are circulated or orbited in the Small Heavenly Circle ritual.

The spinal cord channel (Governor Channel) runs from the perineum to the crown of the head. It is masculine or yang. The Functional Channel runs from the crown of the head, down through the forehead, the palate, the throat, the heart, the solar plexus, the navel, the genitals and ends at the perineum. This channel is considered yin or feminine.

Circuiting the ka'aba represents the harmonious blending of yin and yang. For masculine oriented cultures like that of the Arabs, kissing the Black Stone symbol of Mother Hagar represents coming to terms, at least, with the feminine principle in spirituality.

Hagar is a form of the Egyptian goddess of love, Het-Heru (Hathor). Thus another meaning of kissing the Black Stone is the elevation and refinement of the sexual principle in religion.

Remember, Hagar was an Egyptian. Ka'aba is a compound of three Egyptian psychospiritual words: Ka, Ab and Ba.

The Ka is the personality or the lower self.
The Ab is the will and moral self.
The Ba is the divine self.

Ka-ab-ba is the unification of the three primary parts of the human spirit.

Published by: Fatir Publishing Text is copyright © 2014 Amir Fatir

The ka-aba is veiled as a sign that the feminine principle in religion had been veiled up even as Arab women wear a veil.

Since Hagar was an Egyptian, it is understandable that many Egyptian words would enter into Arabic since she is the black mother of the Arabs and children learn to speak their mother tongue. According to the Bible history, Ishmael was half-Egyptian (i.e., half-African).

The actual meaning of the myth is that Arab culture and knowledge descended from ancient Egypt.

A mixed multitude ("Arabs") went up also with them.

- Exodus 12:38

The well of Zam Zam in the Hajj ritual symbolizes the male seminal fluid. Retention of it preserves health and youth, thus it is "the fountain of youth."

Summary of Meaning of the Five Pillars

In the five pillar formula, the Muslim initiate first witnesses the letters (muqatta'at), the sound vibrations operating in her hands. The highest form of witnessing is via sight.

You will see it with certainty of sight.

-- Quran 102:7

Next the Muslim yogi activates the kundalini or salaat force which directs those mantras to his objective.

Then the Muslim yogi thoroughly purifies his body-mind-spirit complex granting her greater health to increase the salaat force.

Then he abstains from sex to improve his mastery of the body and supplement his salaat energy.

Finally, the initiate utterly conquers his body and mind, bringing it into complete peace (salaam) and submission (Islam) to Allah with the reward of out-of-body projection (Hajj).

At that point he can wear the title Al-Hajj.

Al-Qalaam: The Oracle of the Quran

Human beings are designed in such a way that we are virtually incapable of consciously doing evil to others. Yet we live in a world in which we wrong one another daily.

The Quran teaches that humans are "created in the best of molds." The fundamental human nature is peaceful, righteous, kind-spirited and good.. Yet human beings also possess the ability to rationalize and when we rationalize the actions we think we should take, based upon circumstances as we perceive them, then we are capable of harming others. However, we harm another only after we have given ourselves the rationalization that we are accomplishing or attempting to accomplish something good.

Some examples of pure evil which can be wrought after the mind rationalizes that the evil actions it plans are "for the greater good" include:

1. An expectant mother aborts her baby because she rationalizes that she should not bring a child into a world such as this. The same woman may stridently call for the death penalty for someone who murders a child outside the womb but rationalizes that her own complicity in the murder of her own fetus was "for the greater good."

2. A man sells drugs to others and rationalizes that "they were gonna buy it anyway," so why shouldn't he make money and perhaps even do some good in the community with the drug money he's made.

3. A government and church authorize and bless the buying and selling of slaves under the rationalization that the slaves will be "brought to Jesus in Christianity and civilized so that their souls may go to heaven."

4. A man beats up his wife "for her own good" and rationalizes that "she needs a strong man who won't take no shit to control her."

I will certainly make evil fair-seeming to them.

Published by: Fatir Publishing Text is copyright © 2014 Amir Fatir

-- Quran 15:39

The rationalizing faculty was to be used to bring light to humanity, but when it becomes corrupt, it becomes Satanic and Luciferian. Among other things, Lucifer represents the corruption of the human rationalizing faculty.

How art thou fallen from heaven,
O Lucifer. How art thou fallen down
to the ground?

-- Isaiah

Because it is so easy to do great evil "in the name of God," the ancients devised a fool-proof means of actually determining God's will for every life situation.

The means they devised concerns the consultation of oracles.

Oracles are mentioned in many places in the Bible. Every religion posses an oracle system, including al-Islam.

An oracle reveals God's actual will, not what we might rationalize God's will to be.

When a person learns God's will via an oracle then she can act according to that will and truly function as a Muslim, i.e. one who surrenders her will to do the will of Allah.

An oracle not only reveals God's will, but it also reveals the spiritual shaping forces (angels) involved in the undertaking or event. Knowledge of those shaping factors enables us to invoke their assistance and guidance in our undertaking.

For spiritual technological purposes, an oracle will indicate the appropriate God names, archangels, angels, planets, elementals and the proper mantras and colors to employ to assure the successful attainment of the objective.

An oracle reading will also indicate the areas of vulnerability and the opposing forces involved in the undertaking.

Well-known oracles include the Tarot, Metu Neter, Ifa and I Ching. There are 64 hexagrams (statements) in the I Ching. Those Hexagrams cover every possible situation in life. The Tarot's Major Arcana ("Big Secret") contains 22 statements (cards). It is part of the same oracular system as the I Ching, but the Tarot is incomplete.

Read in the name of your Lord who created.
He created man from a clinging thing.
Read and your Lord is most generous.
He taught with the Oracle [al-Qalaam].
He taught the man what he otherwise could never have known.

-- Quran 96:1-5

The above five verses are the very first revelation of the Quran to Muhammad. The "name" of the Lord which Muhammad is commanded to read refers to the mantras of God.

"Al-Qalaam" is usually translated "pen" or "lot" as in Surah 3 where it states: "Thou wast not with them when they cast their lots to determine which of them would have charge of Maryam."

The world qalaam originally meant "feather" and because early pens were made out of feathers, it became the word used for pen. But feather was an ancient symbol of the oracle because Tehuti, the aspect of God who creates and reveals oracles, is depicted holding a quill and the information of the oracle is the "writings of the heavenly realms." The wings of the bird became a symbol for the heavenly realm because birds can fly to the heavens and because their keen eyesight enables them to see in broader scope from the high vantage point of flight than usual sight can see. That bird sight became a symbol for spiritual vision.

Nun! By the Oracle and what they write.
-- Quran 68:1

The oracle of the Quran was lost. It's title is the Feather of Osiris. Osiris is the Greek rendering of the Egyptian God Ausar. He is referred to in the Quran as 'Asr.

By 'Asr -- surely the man was lost.

-- Quran 103:1

This ayat refers to the losing of the great Quranic oracle, the Feather of Osiris.

The Feather of Osiris is based upon three levels of meanings of the 14 Arabic Mystic Letters which precede 29 Surahs of the Quran. All together they make up 42 statements which, when combined with the 22 Tarot statements of the Major Arcana, 64 statements are provided which equal the 64 hexagrams of the I Ching.

The oracle teaches man what he could otherwise never have known because in using the oracle, mantras are employed and those mantras open the initiate up to knowledge that descends from the higher planes.

The knowledge received via the oracle is called Hikmat in the Quran and Chokmah in the Qaballah system which the Jews adopted from the ancient Canaanite people. Chokmah is the name of the second Tree of Life Sphere, the sphere of Tehuti.

The 42 cards of the Feather of Osiris accord with the 42 assessors in the Hall of Maat. They also accord with the 42 nomes of ancient Egypt.

Oracles work because the random shuffling of cards or casting of shells, etc., is influenced by the individual's subtle life force (the "deity" Ra in Egyptian religion). This force is subtly influenced by the Sun, Moon and planets.

So in casting an oracle, the celestial intelligence (angels) is involved in the "random" selection. The pressure of the pulse, minute secretions of perspiration, the activity of the breath all impact upon the cutting and shuffling of the cards. The card thus selected signifies the will of Allah, not the preference of the seeker.

In the Egyptian system, Ra's boat represented the activity of the sympathetic and parasympathetic nervous systems. Ra's daylight boat was called the Atet boat while His night boat was called Af ("Flesh"). The Atet boat represents the timed progression of the sympathetic nervous system when it has supremacy over the parasympathetic. Then the night comes and the Af boat (parasympathetic) reaches supremacy over the sympathetic.

We have made the Night and Day (two of Our) signs.

-- Quran 17:12

The Egyptians had 12 hours of the night rituals that were based upon the movement of Ra's boat through the Tuat. The Tuat represents the time frame that the parasympathetic is over the sympathetic. Because prayers were offered for the Tuat, the Arabic word for prayer, "Dua," was adapted from "Tuat."

The point of the Sun's angle called 'Asr (Ausar) is the midpoint or point of perfect equilibrium between the sympathetic (Atef boat) and the parasympathetic (Af boat). It is because of that perfect balance (mean) between these two aspects of the autonomic system -- indicated by the equilibrium between night and day -- the 'Asr salaat is said to be the best salaat in Islam.

Guard over the salaat
and the salaat al-wusta
and rise up to Allah
devout.
-- Quran 2:238

In his commentary on this passage, Yusuf Ali wrote: "The Middle Prayer: Salat al wusta: may be translated 'the best or most excellent prayer.' Authorities differ as to the exact meaning of this phrase. The weight of authorities seem to be in favour of interpreting this as the 'Asr prayer (in the middle of the afternoon). [Footnote # 271]

The wusta salaat is indeed the 'Asr salaat but it more deeply represents the energy that runs up the middle of the spine and down the middle of the front of the body (The Functional Channel in Taoism). It is "guarded over" by sealing the points of the energy's escape by the practice of yogic bandhas (activities that close off openings for pranic force). The middle channels of the salaat (kundalini) are the most significant or most excellent channels. They are also the first channels the initiate learns to open in salaat/kundalini development.

The word I've translated "devout" above also signifies a person who has mastered the power of his or her sexual force. As this force is important in raising salaat/kundalini, the Quran says "And rise up to Allah celebate."

The boats of Ra are symbolic. The great priests of Ra in ancient Kamit (Egypt) never thought an actual boat flew across the sky. They knew that the apparent movement of the Sun influenced the nervous system in predictable ways. This movement was symbolized as a boat floating across the sky or flowing through the river (symbolic of the human blood system) of the Tuat and in other literature as floating through the celestial ocean called Nut.

Behold! In the creation
Of the heavens and the earth;
In the alternation
Of the Night and the Day;
In the sailing of the ships
Through the Ocean
For the profit of mankind;
In the rain which Allah
Sends down from the skies,
And the life which He gives therewith
To an earth that is dead;
In the beasts of all kinds
That He scatters
Through the earth;
In the change of the winds,
And the clouds which they
Trail like their slaves
Between the sky and the earth --
(Here) indeed are Signs
For a people that are wise.

-- Quran 2:164

Published by: Fatir Publishing Text is copyright © 2014 Amir Fatir

Yusuf Ali Translation

The "ships" referred to above represent the same principle as the Egyptian boat of Ra.

The Tuat was depicted as a circle made of the body of Osiris. Osiris is pictured in a yoga pose with his legs bent behind him so that his feet touch his head. This hieroglyph represents the sealing in of the Ra force energy so that it flows in a cycle. This is the advanced microcosmic orbit of the Taoist yoga which circulates the Chi (salaat) energy in a cycle. The Egyptians depicted the same process by showing a snake curved with his tail in his mouth. The snake is the creative serpent power (kundalini). The tail in the snake's mouth represents the closing off of any passage for the energy to leak out via mudras and bandhas which are learned and practiced in yoga. The circle also represents the circulation of the Ra/salaat force.

The snake is usually shown encircling the Sun disk as a sign that the sun is the source of the salaat/kundalini energy.

The same spiritual scientific principle was coded in the Arabic Letter Miym (m).

م

Two forms of the Arabic letter Miym

The astrological glyph for Leo which is ruled by the Sun, is the same as the Arabic letter Miym.

Picture
The Egyptian hieroglyph for the letter M is an owl. The owl signifies night vision or spiritual insight as the Ra force for spiritual meditative work is most accessible at night.

In the Feather of Osiris oracle, Miym signifies Heru Khenti-an-maati (Heru the Blind) which is the awakened state of consciousness derived from ignoring (being blind to) the emotional influences. It's element is fire.

Chant: I seek refuge with the Lord of men
King of men

Published by: Fatir Publishing Text is copyright © 2014 Amir Fatir

God of men
From the evil whispering of the khanaas
Which whispers through the hearts of men
From the jinn an the men

-- Quran Surah 114

A khanaas (also called Khansa) is the global consciousness or accumulation of all thoughts, feelings, ideas and emotions on a planet. The collection of psychic data is not static. It can unconsciously influence humans via the heart chakra. When an evil impression enters a person's mind, it is depicted as the "evil whispering of the khanaas." It is symbolized as a whisper because the information or suggestion thus imparted is accomplished beneath the breath or very subtly. The victim of such an evil suggestion usually thinks the evil thought, feeling, idea or urge is his own when it has actually descended from the mass accumulated consciousness. This web of consciousness is also referred to as Illiyin and Illiyun (Yang and Yin) in the Quran, but this information is, of course, coded and kept secret from those who cannot decipher Quranic code.

Chanting of mantras and prayers, as well as the singing of hymns, is important because such activities serve to counteract the negative whispers within the khanaas. If righteous people were to flood the global environment with words of power, the evil whispering of the khanaas would be thwarted and the crazy thoughts that spur people's insane (possessed) behaviour would diminish.

The three khansaas are codified in the above Surah as: 1) Rabbi-n-naas (Evolved beings or "Lord of the people"), 2) Maliki-n-naas or Malaki-n-naas (Angelic beings or King of the people) and 3) Ilaahi-n-naas (Divine beings or God of the people).

In astrology they correspond to mutable (Rabb), Fixed (Malik) and Cardinal (Ilaah) signs.

Humans are evolved beings (Rabbi-n-naas) because we have evolved from lower forms and are evolving still.

The beast or animal residue in humanity remains bodily as the Reptilian Brain (Brain Stem), Mammalian Brain (Limbus) and canine teeth. Present humanity stands at a midpoint in evolution between animal life and true human life. Tehuti refers to the common masses as "beast-men." The next step (which some prophets have already attained) is "man-beast." Eventually the beast content of the human gene pool will be weeded out so that a new kind of humanity will stand forth.

The Quran teaches that Allah will not cease to change our forms "again and again into forms you know not." The evolution of the human being is not yet finished.

The Three Nafs (Souls)

Islam holds that there are three primary states of consciousness. They are called nafs al-ammaarah (the passionate soul), nafs al-lawwamah (the censuring soul) and nafs al-mutma'innah (the soul at rest).

Many teachers hold that these three consciousness levels are actually types of people and it is understandable that if these three nafs are types of consciousness then there would be people who functioned primarily at one of them.

The ideas concerning nafs al-ammaarah are derived from this verse:

I do not exculpate myself. Lo! the (human) soul enjoineth unto evil, save that whereon my Lord hath mercy. Lo! my Lord is Forgiving, Merciful.

-- Quran 12:54
Mohammed Marmaduke Pickthall Translation

The ideas concerning nafs al-lawwamah are derived from this verse:

Nay, I swear by the accusing soul.

-- Quran 7:52
Mohammed Marmaduke Pickthall Translation

The ideas concerning nafs al-mutma'innah are derived from this verse:

But ah! thou soul at peace!
Return unto thy Lord, content in His good pleasure!
Enter thou among My bondmen!
Enter thou My Garden!

-- Quran 89:27-30

The three nafs actually indicate stages in the meditation process. In our ordinary state of consciousness our minds (nafs or plural, anfus) are commanded by sensory input from the environment, random thoughts, feelings, the contents of our blood, emotional complexes and engrams. Moreover, we are commanded by our own passions. The Muslim initiate learns to take advantage of those passions and use them to fuel his ascension. The salaat force is integrally related to the sexual drive. Rather than initially trying to extinguish that drive, the initiate learns to utilize it to fuel and empower his meditation. This can lead to reaching a state called ecstatic trance which, in the Quran, is called "the garden of bliss."

When the initiate feels the energy of the passionate soul (nafs al-ammarrah), he focuses on the passion and uses it to raise his mental vibrational rate. He is not compelled to ease the tension by having a quick orgasm, rather he recognizes that the passion he is experiencing is an addition to his usual energy field.

Sexual passion can actually be invigorating and can be a catalyst for feeling and thus becoming younger. That feeling of being younger reminds the cellular memory of its former, youthful state of health and many times the body can spontaneously heal itself. When Marvin Gaye sang about sexual healing, he was touching upon this kind of concept.

People in love always feel young and therefore they act younger, do the things young people do and are thus open for a rejuvenation of their bodies. It doesn't matter if the woman in love is 87, once she falls in love she starts feeling more like a girl again.

The Muslim initiate focuses on his or her passion and then circulates it first up the spine and then around the entire body.

Published by: Fatir Publishing Text is copyright © 2014 Amir Fatir

Nafs al-lawammah indicates that the next stage in meditation in which the initiate censures or cuts off her thoughts. Nafs al-lawammah is not the "accusing soul," it is the censuring soul. It's connection with the resurrection of the kundalini force is indicated by the preceding verse which says, "Nay, I swear by the Day of Resurrection" (yawm al-qiyaamat). This is also code for the resurrection of the life force (salaat).

The initiate censures or cuts off all thoughts that enter her field of consciousness. She doesn't allow a thought to continue into a sentence and doesn't allow sentences to reproduce into many sentences. If, for example, she is meditating and finds herself wondering, "Gosh, I hope I can make my car note this month," she will, instead, cut the thought off before it can complete itself. She might terminate that thought at "Gosh, I hope I..." After some time of terminating thoughts the mind will empty itself of all thinking and true consciousness behind the outer consciousness can emerge.

One of the reasons of practicing dhikr (jappa in yoga) is that the circular repetition of the words of power facilitates the left hemisphere of the brain's giving up its linear mode of thinking. The initiate dhikrs for example, "Haaaaaaa Meeeeemmmmmmmmm" over and over and this circular mode of mental communication breaks the mind out of bondage to the left brain's need to make sentences.

Eventually, out of censuring thought, the initiate reaches the state of consciousness called nafs al-mutma'innah (the rested soul).

It is at this point that no thoughts are in the mental field and the initiate finds himself conscious of being conscious.

The initiate can then experience the unity of her true self with Allah (Tauhid) and reach that rested, peaceful state of superconsciousness that is called samadhi.

The mind is thus liberated and not squeezed into the artificial prison cell of identification with one body and one time period. It can then transcend its body and spread out to infinity. This infinity (in time as well as space) is the "Garden" the Quran speaks so often of. The Quran says that the Garden is as wide as the entire heavens and the earth. When the mind,

Published by: Fatir Publishing Text is copyright © 2014 Amir Fatir

through meditation, reaches nafs al-mutma'innah, then it expands to infinity.

Tantric Yoga

The ancients recognized that the very life of the universe itself was a sexual force. This sexuality of the universe can be observed in the polarities between the Sun and Moon, electrons and protons, and the male and female divisions in all living things including plants. Within the human body there are balancing polarities of yang (masculine) and yin (feminine) forces. The left hemisphere of the brain is masculine while the right is feminine.

Rather than attempt to block or subdue the sexual urge, the ancients sought to harmonize and civilize it and to utilize the awesome power of sex to promote a person's ascension into a divine state of consciousness (Ilaahi-n-naas).

The ancients developed tantric yoga as the means by which to harness, harmonize and utilize the sexual force.

Tantric yoga has been called sex yoga and it indeed incorporates sexual principles and practices. But sex is more a means tantrists use to achieve yoga (unity with God or Tauhid) than an end to itself. While tantric practices can indeed augment sexual pleasure and enable practitioners to perform unbelievable sexual feats, even the pleasure derived from sex is channeled into spiritual directions. Tantric yoga is not a practice of hedonism although hedonists would do well to use their natural abilities for spiritual ends rather than simply "getting off" on bodily pleasures.

The force that yogis use is called shakti in Sanskrit, shekinah in Hebrew and sakana in the Quran.

And among His Signs is that He created for
you mates from your own souls for you to
activate the sakana with them.
And He has placed between you love and
compassion. Surely in that are miracles
for people who meditate.

-- Quran 30:21

In the above ayat, I have translated "taskunuw" (the plural verb in the second person of "sakana") "activate the sakana" (which is the same as shakti). Others have translated the same words to mean "that ye might find quiet of mind with them" and "that ye may dwell in tranquillity with them." For externally directed students, those translations are fine. But for those seeking the inner and truer meaning of Quranic revelation, "activate the shakti" is more in accord with the technical meaning of sakana, shechinah and shakti.

Proper application of the techniques of tantric yoga enable the partners to perform actual miracles (ayats) and many of the sexual feats are performed in a meditative state. Thus the Quran says, "There are miracles in that for those who meditate." The word "ayat" (miracles) could also be translated "signs" and in the entire verse are signs regarding tantric yoga.

The following technical terms are all similar:

Sakana
Shakti
Shekinah
Ra
Libido
Orgone
Salaat
Kundalini

The various scriptural personalities who symbolize tantric yoga include:

Nephthys
Het-Heru
Mary of Magdalene
Queen of Sheba
Venus
Aphrodite
Kali
Dakini
Astarte
Isis

Neith
Jezebel

Where persons can use sex individually for spiritual ascension, tantric yoga is properly performed by two people.

Tantra actually means "weaving" as a symbol of how the bodies of two people weave in and out and, more accurately, how the energies of the two initiates can move into the other party so that the male can experience female sexuality (not just partake of it) and the woman can experience male sexuality.

And be not like a woman who breaks into untwisted
strands the yarn she has spun after it has become strong.

-- Quran 16:92
Yusuf Ali Translation

The "yarn" in the above verse refers to the spiritual sexual thread of tantric sex that has been split up and made strong between a woman and her husband if they are both initiates.

One of the primary meanings of the Egyptian goddess Neith (Nit or Net) is "she who weaves." This goddess was one of the original archetypes of tantric yoga.

A Lost-Found Lesson of the Nation of Islam states that the duty of the M.G.T.-G.C.C. (female members of the Nation) is "to sew, cook and in general how to act at home and abroad." The "sewing" refers symbolically to tantric sexual yoga. This is a word that is telling women Muslims to learn to master the tantric arts and thereby learn how to "civilize the general" (their husbands) via sex. (G.C.C. means General Civilization Class.)

Your wives are a tilth unto you.
So enter your tilth however
You please. And send before something for
Your souls and be conscious of Allah and
know that are to meet Him.
And give good news to the believers.

Published by: Fatir Publishing Text is copyright © 2014 Amir Fatir

-- Quran 2:223

A tilth is cultivated land in which a farmer places his seeds. The women here are likened to that tilth -- physically the planting of the semen (seeds) inside them but on a deeper plane it refers to the depositing of words of power (hekau or mantras) inside the trance state of consciousness.

In tantric yoga are many positions for sexual intercourse which are designed to augment pleasure as well as to activate the shakti energy for specific purposes. For example, if the purpose of the sexual act was to send healing power to the wife's father, then she would mount her husband on top with her back facing him.

If the purpose of the sexual act was for her to reach a state of trance so that she could prophesy, then she might hook her legs over the back of the sofa and lean down so that the blood would rush to her head while the husband brought sexual pleasure to her.

All of the asanas and mudras of hatha yoga were originally intended to forestall orgasm and to heighten the sexual power of the initiates. For example in the lotus pose (qada'ah in salaat) the heal of the woman is pressed against her clitoris. This is to enable her to achieve sexual pleasure when, as trance onsets, the natural rocking of the body creates a rubbing against her clitoris from her heel.

The breathing and mudras were intended to allow the male to hold onto his orgasm for incredibly long period of time and then to redirect (via the mudra) the orgasm up his spine and ultimately to his brain.

The Bible book entitled "Song of Solomon" is actually a tantric text that depicts the spiritual lovemaking between Solomon and Sheba. A kind of preface to that book is found in the story of Solomon and Sheba in the Quran.

It was said to her, enter the palace.
So when she saw it she thought it was a lake of
water and she uncovered her legs. He said:
This is but a palace paved with glass.

-- Quran 27:44

The Queen of Sheba and Solomon entered the glass palace of Solomon. This is deep code language for the elevation of the energy of sexual yoga to the region of the brain that the Taoists refer to as "the Crystal Palace."

The Crystal Palace is the brain region that included the thalamus, pineal gland, pituitary glad and hypothalamus.

Mantak Chia has written: "Once the Crystal Palace is open, it becomes illuminated like millions of shining crystals. It can give and receive light and awaken our inner knowledge and deepest potentials. It receives light and knowledge from the universe and reflects it to the various organs and glands to enhance them. The Crystal Palace also has 10 holes connected to 10 Celestial Stems, which in Chinese astrology regulate all heavenly energies that influence the earth."

It should be mentioned here that the concept of Sulayman (Solomon) came from Persia where they have 10 sulaymans who are considered to be demi-gods. The 10 sulaymans relate to the 10 Celestial Stems of Taoist yoga.

As a summation of the revealed books and principles before it, the Quran expects the reader to have been made familiar with the principles to which it refers and therefore doesn't explain any of them in detail. It is expected that the initiate was already familiar with the concepts and the Quran clarifies them and adds "extra credit" information for true students. However, without an understanding of the previous revelations, a reader of the Quran would be lost indeed when it comes to comprehending the deep spiritual wisdom contained within the Quran.

The Tree of Life

The Qaballah is the esoteric wisdom of the ancient people of Canaan. Its origin is Egyptian.

There were no vowels or diacritical marks in the early written copies of the Quran.

Published by: Fatir Publishing Text is copyright © 2014 Amir Fatir

When the quran refers to the qiblah, it is actually referring to the Qaballah.

Qaballah means to "Face Allah" or to undergo the initiation necessary to come "face to face with Allah."

Egyptian mythology says that Ausar (Osiris) was buried in a tree in Syria. This is a sign of the fact that the Syrians (Canaanites) received the Tree of Life from Ausarian priests of Egypt. But the Tree they received was of the dead god and not the living science.

The tree of life also in the midst of the garden, and
the tree of knowledge of good and evil.

- Genesis 2:9

The Jews got their Qaballah knowledge from the Canaanites. Which is why the Bible says "Thy father was a Canaanite."

So in learning the Qaballah from the Canaanites, the Jews actually gained second hand Egyptian knowledge.

The fools among the people will say: What hath turned
them from the Qiblah to which they were used?" Say:
To Allah belong East and West: He guideth whom he
will to a Way that is straight.

Thus have We made of you an Ummah justly balanced,
that ye might be witnesses over the nations, and the
Messenger a witness over yourselves; and We appointed
the Qiblah to which thou wast used only to test those
who followed the Messenger from those who would turn
on their heels (from the Faith). Indeed it was (a change)
momentous, except to those guided by Allah. And never
would Allah make your faith of no effect. For Allah is
to all people most surely full of kindness, Most Merciful.

-- Quran 2:142-142

Published by: Fatir Publishing Text is copyright © 2014 Amir Fatir

The inner meaning of the above verses is the change of the Qaballah system. The actual change is obscured. The prophet changed from an Arabian Qaballah system to a Canaanite Qaballah system.

The mosque or temple in Jerusalem was built by King Hiram and his architect Hiram-abi (known as Hiram-abith to the Masons). This is the Masjid al Haram (the mosque of Hiram) of the Quran.

In changing the Qaballah (Qiblah) from the one the mystic Arabs were familiar with to the one used by the Jews, controversy arose.

The physical prayer direction was a sign of a more monumental change, the change of Qaballah methods.

The first Qaballah (Qiblah) was actually the heavens. We see the turning of thy face to the heavens. Now We will turn thee to a Qaballah that will satisfy thee."

It was then that the mystic of al-Islam were given the "Temple of Hiram-abi as the symbol of their Qaballistic system. This, of course, included all the secret teachings associated with Freemasonry.

In turning to the Qaballah of Jerusalem, Muhammad was actually seizing control of the wisdom tradition of the ancient people of Canaan as well as the wisdom of ancient Kamit (Egypt).

The Qaballah is comprised of the literal, practical and mystical Qaballah. The hallmark of the mystical Qaballah is the Tree of Life.

The very best book I've read on The Tree of Life is Metu Neter, Vol. I by Ra Un Nefer Amen. Readers are encouraged to read that book for a full comprehension of the Tree of Life.

Sephora (Sphere)	Translation	Egyptian	Principle
0 Ain Soph Ur	Light w/o limit	Amen	Nothingness
1 Kether	Crown	Ausar	Omnipresence
2 Chochmah	Wisdom	Tehuti	Omniscience
3 Binah	Understanding	Khepera	Omnipotence
4 Hesed	Mercy	Maat	Synthesis
5 Giborah	Strength	Herukhuti	Analysis
6 Tifareth	Beauty	Heru	Will
7 Netzack	Power	Het- Heru	Integration
8 Hod	Glory	Sebek	Separation
9 Yesod	Foundation	Auset	Trance
10 Malkuth	Kingdom	Geb	Health/ Earth

The Lord's prayer states, "Thine is the Kingdom, and the Power, and the Glory forever. Amen." Four spheres are slipped into the Gospel to indicate that the writers were familiar with Qaballistic wisdom. "Kingdom," "Power," "Glory," and "Amen" are spheres 10, 7, 8 and 0 respectively.

The "God Name" of sphere 1, Kether, is Eheiah which, in Arabic, is Hayya (Life). Surah 2:255 states that Allah is "al-hayyul qayyuwm." This is a reference to the God Name of Kether. In addition, that verse states that "His throne extends to the heavens and the earth." Thrones is kursiy in Arabic and kursiy is one of the appellations of one of the Tree's spheres. "Al-hayyu-1-qayyum" should be translated, "the rising life force."

The Tree of Life is a cosmogram that graphically depicts the divine methodology, the proper means of doing any deed from creating a universe to making a baby to writing a book.

The cosmogram displays a picture of the cosmology (the science of order).

There are pictures, mantras, chakras, planets, metals, animals and plants that are associated with each sphere of the Tree. The connecting lines of the Tree are called paths. In "pathworking," the initiate learns to travel to various dimensions as represented by the spheres. The spheres are the various "heavens" to which the prophet ascended on his Night Journey.

Published by: Fatir Publishing Text is copyright © 2014 Amir Fatir

In the threeworld systems of Fitrah, Rabbi naas includes spheres 9, 7 and 8. Maliki naas includes spheres 6, 5 and 4. Ilaahi naas includes spheres 3, 2, 1 and 0.

Each card of the Major Arcana Tarot (the true Torah or Tarut of Moses) provides a meditation picture that corresponds with a particular path. Meditation on the appropriate picture permits the initiate to soul travel to that world.

The initiate traveler ("wayfarer" in the Quran) will discover that Allah is indeed the "Lord of all the worlds."

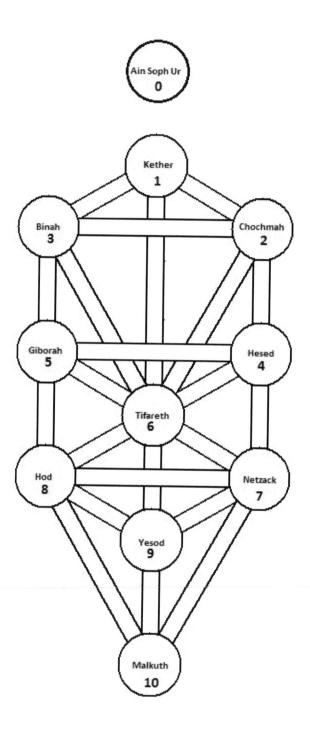

Mother, Son and Holy Ghost

Ruwh is the Quranic term for Spirit. Ruwh refers to the scientific application of yogic breathing. In Sanskrit it is called pranayama.

And seek Allah's protection with the lungs.

-- Quran

Prana means breath or air. But it actually refers to the life force particles in air. Yama means both restraint and lengthening. In the proper practice of pranayama. This serves to lengthen the breathing so that the rate of breathing is slowed. In slowing the breathing, consciousness is introverted.

When the energy of the breathing process causes celestial energy to descend to meet with human spiritual energy, that descending energy is called Ruwh (Ruach in Hebrew).

Yama, incidentally, is the name of the Tibetan god of the underworld (collective subconscious) and corresponds to Ausar. This tells us that pranayama connects the individual consciousness (jivan) with the collective subconscious (atman).

Maryam (Merriam) is the name of Jesus' mother. "Yam," related to "Yama," also means "sea." The sea is a symbol of deep trance. Entering into mediumistic trance often feels as if you are going underwater.

Pranayama enables the initiate to enter trance (Mary) and then the higher spirit (Ruwh) connects with the trance state. This is referred to as "the virgin became pregnant with child." The "virgin" represents the state of trance consciousness.

To give you a perfect boy.

-- Quran 19:19

A new energy of consciousness develops from the union of the Ruwh (spirit) with the trance condition (Maryam). This new consciousness is symbolized as the son of that spirit as well as the son of trance (Jesus son of Mary) because it was trance and the activation of spirit energy that produced the Awakened state of Consciousness.

This is among the hidden wisdom of Tauhid (yoga) that's embedded in the Quran.

Reincarnation

The yoga principle called karma is expressed in the Quran as qadr and qadiy. Qadr is usually translated "power" and qadiy is often translated "judgement." But qadiy is the karmic sentence a person received in a life or accumulation of lives while qadr stands for the abilities or "powers" (called "virtues" in the New Testament) a person has gained due to her struggles across lifetimes. The sum or "balance sheet" of qadr/qadiy is "diyn," the "path" of reincarnation.

It is the principle of Islam that all living beings will eventually return to Allah.

How can you cover the truth about Allah when you were dead then He reanimated you then He Kills you then revives you again then you return to Him.

-- Quran 2:28

Frequently, the Quran speaks of "raising the dead." The resurrection of the dead represents reincarnation.

Not only can life reincarnate into higher forms, but people can reincarnate into lower forms of life.

And ye know those of you who broke the Sabbath, how We said unto them: Be ye apes, despised and hated!

-- Quran 2:65
Pickthall Translation

In another place, the people who disobeyed Moses are transformed into apes and pigs.

Surah 91 indicates that Allah "has no fear of the consequences." In other words, despite how long it takes, all life will eventually return to Allah. It is that that is predestined -- that we will grow into becoming one with Allah. The Quran says, "We said to the heavens and the earth, come willingly or come unwillingly." Not only organic life will "come to Allah," but so also must the life that is considered inanimate.

The Quran tells people to "remember" this and that. The remembrance intended is that of past lives and agreements made in those lives. Chanting dhikrs facilitates the remembrance of past lives. One who can remember many lives is called a "shaykh" (literally, "old man"). He is "old" in that his consciousness goes back to olden times.

People who can remember all their lives are called "al-khaliduwn," the immortal ones. The are immortal because their consciousness does not end when their bodies return to dust.

The ancient Egyptian masters knew how to pre-determine who they'd be in the next life an some of them buried treasures which they intended to unearth when they reincarnated later. This was the origin of the quest for buried treasure.

You can take it with you.

The Akashic Record

The yogis of India believed that there is a record or book that records every action, thought and emotion in a subtle substance called "akashia." This record contains all information of the past as well as the future. This Book is called "the Akashic Record."

In the Quran this book is called "the book of Allah," "the Mother of the Books," "the Clear Book," and "book that leaves out nothing, small or great."

The Akashic Record is coded under the Mystic Letters Alif Laam Miym (A.L.M.) in the Quran.

Alif Laam Miym.

That is the Book.
Never doubt in it,
It is a guidance for
The God-realized ones.

-- Quran 2:1-2

Meditation permits the initiate to access portions of the Akashic Record and thereby have true knowledge of the past and the future.

Nor is there aught of the Unseen in the heaven or earth,
but it is (recorded) in a clear record.

-- Quran 27:75
Y. Ali Translation

Knowest thou not that Allah knows all that is in the
heaven and on earth? Indeed it is all in a record,
and that is easy for Allah.

-- Quran 36:12

No misfortune can happen on earth or in your souls
but is recorded in a Book before We bring it into existence:
Surely that is easy for Allah.

-- Quran 57:22

The word translated "record" or "book" in the above verses is "kitaab" in Arabic which means any kind or recorded document whether on paper or computer disk or any subtler type of recording medium such as akashia.

Allah's 99 Names

Catholics use a rosary comprised of 108 beads. Some yogis use 1080 meditation beads. Muslims use 99 dhkir beads, each bead symbolizing one of Allah's 99 names (attributes).

The reality of each system is that the name of the deity symbolizes an attribute of the one God, not a multiplicity of gods. This is true for yoga, Egyptian religion, Buddhism, Taoism and Islam.

It is as wrong for Muslims to accuse other systems of a multiplicity of gods as it would be for others to accuse Muslims of worshipping 99 gods.

Each of Allah's 99 names is to be used in dhikr (jappa, i.e. repetition) to call forth that particular attribute that accords with a particular need. For example, if a Muslim needed a husband, she would dhikr (chant) "al-wadood," (the Beloved). Al-mughniy (the enricher) would be chanted for money.

An aspect of the Qaballah is gematria, the science of working with numerical values. In gematria (part of the literal Qaballah) numbers are added across to learn their root numerical value. For example, the number 379 would become 3+7+9 = 19 - 1+9 = 10 = 1+0 = 1. So 379 conceals the numerical value of one.

Rosary beads 108 (conceals the number 18)

Meditation beads 1080 (conceals the number 18)

Dhikr beads 99 (conceals the number 18)

In the Eastern hemisphere, 18 was discovered to be the average number of breaths per minute taken by human beings.

The 9+9 attributes of Allah conceals an instruction for the meditator to focus on her breathing while chanting.

1080 = 1+0+8 = 9

108 = 1+0+8 = 9

99 = 9+9 = 18 = 1+8 = 9

Proper focus on the chanting/breathing formula will result in the meditator falling into the state of trance that's symbolized by the 9th sphere of the Tree of Life.

Dhikring until trance is achieved gives power to the meditator so that his chanting bears fruit. Then he is known as "al-siddiyq," i.e., the one whose words become true.

Conclusion

The yoga of Islam (Tauhid) can be experienced by applying yogic principles of Quranic tenets.

Each step or limb or yoga requires training and effort, but the reward for the person who perseveres is immense.

The following list of suggested readings contain the information that will enable the reader to learn basic yogic techniques to begin the practice of Tauhid.

Suggested Readings

Iyeneger, Light on Yoga
Amen, Ra Un Nefer, Meter Neter Vol. I
Ali, Muhammad, The Holy Quran
Ali, Yusuf, The Holy Quran
Fatir, Amir, Why Does Muhammad & Any Muslim "Murder the Devil?
Fatir, Amir, Tantric Sex magic Rituals for Modern Black Women
Avalon, Aruth, The Serpent Power
Sivananda, Any book in his yoga series
Chia, Mantak, Awaken the Healing Light of the Tao
Chia, Mantak, Taoist Secrets of Love
Any book by Professor *Hilton Hotema*

Published by: Fatir Publishing Text is copyright © 2014 Amir Fatir

<u>Other Books by Amir</u>

The Black Angles – Soon to be re-released check website
The Egyptian Tree of Life – Available on website in ebook form
Salaat al-Wusta The Middle Pillar - Soon to be released check website
Why Does Muhammad and Any Muslim Murder the Devil? – Soon to be re-released check website

New titles will be made available on the website as they are released.

Contact
www.amirfatir.com
info@amirfatir.com

Published by: Fatir Publishing Text is copyright © 2014 Amir Fatir

Made in the USA
San Bernardino, CA
25 October 2017